Marrriage Dynamics

Marrriage Dynamics

Dr Francis Madzivadondo

Chikavhu Publications

CONTENTS

CONTENTS

First Printing, 2022

Acknowledgements

Thanks for this book must be given and expressed to my dear wife Sandra and my children, Evans, Blessing, Nyasha, Tinotenda and Tinashe and their children for the encouragement they gave me as I was writing this book. They provided a conducive atmosphere that allowed me to be able to hear from God and to be able to write the book. My son law Mustafa for helping with the final touches and publishing the book.

Professor E.H. Guti and Doctor Eunor Guti the Apostles of Jesus Christ, the founders of Forward In Faith Ministries International for mentoring me into a minister of Jesus Christ of whom I am today. I thank them for their patience with me over the years as I was growing in the work of the ministry. Forward in Faith Ministries International church in Lubumbashi DRC. This is where my journey as an author began. Most of the stuff in the book I first taught it to this church (FIF Lubumbashi) as the Lord was giving it to me. Thank you for all the support you gave me. Forward In Faith Ministries International Brisbane Australia, thank you for your support, those prayer bands we used to do together. I give all the glory to my Father God who has allowed me to minister to other people through this book. Thank you for showing me some of the hidden things about marriage.

| 2 |

2 |

Introduction

Ephesians 5: 20-33

Giving thanks always for all things unto God and the Father in the name of our Lord Jesus Christ; Wives submit yourselves unto your own husbands, as unto the Lord. For the husband is the head of the wife, even as Christ is the head of the church: and he is the saviour of the body. Therefore as the church is subject unto Christ, so let the wives be to their own husbands in everything. Husbands, love your wives, even as Christ also loved the church, and gave himself for it; That he might sanctify and cleanse it with the washing of water by the word. That he might present it to himself a glorious church, not having a spot, or wrinkle, or any such thing; but that it should be holy and without blemish. So ought men to love their wives as their own bodies. He that loveth his wife loveth himself. For no man ever hated his own flesh; but nourisheth and cherisheth it, even as the Lord the church:[For we are members of his body, of his flesh, and of his bones. For this cause shall a man leave his father and mother, and shall be joined unto his wife, and they two shall be one flesh.This is a great mystery: but I speak concerning Christ and the church. Nevertheless let every one of you in particular so love his wife even as himself, and the wife sees that she reverence her husband.

Marriage is a covenant that is entered by a man, and a woman before God.It is a life covenant, only to be broken by death or fornication. Matthew 5:32 *But I say unto you, That whosoever shall put away his wife, saving for the cause of fornication, causeth her to commit adultery: and whosoever shall marry her that is divorced committeth* adultery. Mark 10:6-10 *But from the beginning of the creation, God made them male and female. For this cause shall a man leave his father and mother, and cleave to his wife; And they twain, but one flesh. What therefore God hath joined together, let not man put asunder. And in the house his disciples asked him again of the same matter.*

Marriage is a spiritual institution which God ordained in the garden of Eden. Genesis 2:20-25*And Adam gave names to all cattle, and to the fowl of the air, and to every beast of the field; but for Adam, there was not found a help meet for him. And the Lord God caused a deep sleep to fall upon Adam, and he slept: and he took one of his ribs, and closed up the flesh instead thereof; And the rib, which the Lord God had taken from man, made he a woman, and brought her unto the man. [And Adam said, This is now bone of my bones, and flesh of my flesh: she shall be called a woman because she was taken out of a man. Therefore shall a man leave his father and his mother, and shall cleave unto his wife: and they shall be one flesh. And they were both naked, the man and his wife, and were not ashamed.*

Marriage must be lived according to the principles of God. The fundamental laws of marriage are love, forgiveness, patience, submission, and long-suffering. Galatians 5:22 *But the fruit of the spirit is love, joy, peace, longsuffering, gentleness, goodness, faith. The principles are the fruit of the Holy Spirit. It then follows that a woman or man without the Holy Spirit working in him cannot live a biblical successful marriage life. Marriage is divine, and it is a mystery, it is not man's idea.* Ephesians 5:31-32 *For this cause shall a man leave his father and mother and shall be joined unto his wife, and they two shall be one flesh. This is a great mystery:*

but I speak concerning Christ and the church. It is mystery, meaning that no man has full understanding of what it is all about, there is need for revelation from God for us to be able to understand it and to enjoy it.

God started marriage for man to have a companion, a helper and for his reproduction. Genesis 2:20 -23 *And Adam gave names to all cattle, and to the fowl of the air, and to every beast of the field; but for Adam there was not found an help meet for him, And the Lord God caused a deep sleep to fall upon Adam, and he slept: and he took one of his ribs, and closed up the flesh instead thereof; And the rib, with which the Lord God had taken from a man, made he a woman, and brought her unto the man. And Adam said, this is now bone of my bones, and flesh of my flesh; she shall be called woman, because she was taken out of man.* Genesis 1:28 *And God blessed them, and God said unto them, be fruitful, and multiply, and replenish the earth, and subdue it: and have dominion over the fish of the sea, and over the fowl of the air, and over every living thing that moveth upon the earth.*

All bible quotations in this book are from the King James Version.

3

What does it take to have a good marriage?

There is no ready-made marriage and a good marriage does not just happen, we do not find good marriages by chance. A good marriage is built upon a sound knowledge of the institution of marriage which was ordained by God in the garden of Eden. You need to get an understanding of how it can be achieved. Proverbs 24:3 -4 *By wisdom a house is built, and by understanding it is established: by knowledge, the rooms are filled with all precious and pleasant riches.*

Marriage is an institution that operates on laws like any other institution. If one cannot master those laws disaster will always strike. It is built upon the principles of the word of God. If we are not skillful with the word of God, it follows that we cannot effectively execute the demands of marriage. Many get into marriage with different assumptions about what they think marriage is all about and they quickly get out of it after discovering that what they thought marriage was is not what it is. Building a good biblical marriage demands growth and development on both parties involved. Two totally different people are coming to live together, they are different in everything. There is a gender difference, education, upbringing, the two grew up in totally different environments, they have gone through different experiences as they were growing up. All these things will have an impact on them as they start to live together. When they start to live together they must deal with all the differences that have which we have seen above so that they may be able to fit into each other. It is like in a carpentry workshop where so many tools are used to make different joins fit into each other to form one entity. Many times, it is not easy to have those joins fit into each other.

I am living with someone who has a totally different biological makeup. Men and women think, see, reason and do things differently. "Men and women are different. Not equal in function or needs or position but equal in importance. They have mental differences, men and women think differently. This is due to hormonal and developmental differences that start as the child develops before birth. They have emotional differences. Women are affected by the menstrual cycle, lactation, and pregnancy. The hypothalamus functions differently in women and men. Men operate on sight and visual whereas women operate more on an emotional or feeling level. A man's and a woman's needs and what they expect from marriage are different. If we do not recognize this, we are heading for problem roads in our marriage." Prof. E. H. Guti pages 10-11 Strategies for Saving Marriages for this generation.

If I want to have a prosperous marriage I must first sit down and understand from the maker how the other person has been wired emotionally, physically, and spiritually. I must learn his or her biological makeup, his or her priorities. I must invest time to study my spouse. Ignorance of the differences between men and women is the number one reason why many marriages fail. People spent money and time in school studying so many other things but very few invest time in studying about marriage. Many people get into marriage with absolutely no idea of what they will be doing. They saw others getting married and they saw it as a natural and normal thing to do. After getting into the marriage and encountering things that they never thought they could face they quickly get out of it as quickly as they got into it. They keep on trying, getting in, and out thinking that one day they shall be lucky to get a good wife or husband, they are not aware that there is no good wife or husband. To have a good marriage is a result of hard work of learning and sacrifice, it does not come in a silver platter.

There are unavoidable challenges that people face when they start to live together as husband and wife. Training Is needed to be able to face those challenges and deal with them successfully as they show up. We have people today who are living together but they are not husband and wife, they agree to live together as partners, it is because they do not want to take the responsibility to work out their marriage. They are just living together but they are not committed to each other, each person is doing his or her own things but living together with the other person. They are avoiding becoming one flesh or one person, this is what it means to be married. It is the hard part, to surrender certain things habits, and all for the benefit of the other person.

Ephesians 5:25-27 *Husbands, love your wives, even as Christ also loved the church, and gave himself for it; That he might sanctify and cleanse it with the washing of water by the word, that he might present it to himself a glorious church, not having spot, or wrinkle, or any such thing; but that it should be holy and without blemish. Jesus is busy sanctifying the church, His bride to make her better by each day. Both husband and wife must have the desire to have a good marriage and start to work towards having one.*

In the scriptures above we see how Christ sanctifies and cleanses the church with the washing of water by the word. Christ does not wait to get a glorious church by chance. He has engaged himself in the work of washing it. Jesus is busy preparing for Himself a church with no spot or wrinkle. He is doing the work himself every day. This is what we should be doing every day perfecting our marriages, no one is going to do that for us. The church cannot do that job for you nor the parents of your wife or husband, even God does not do that for us

4

Salvation is fundamental in marriage

No man is born a husband or a wife, we are all born men or women with the potential to become husbands and wives. We can only become husbands and wives through getting married and getting trained. You get married to a boy or a girl and out of them, you must make a wife or husband of your choice. The boy or girl you get married to is just raw material out of which you will get a wife or husband. No one develops that raw material except yourself, failure to develop the raw material leads to divorce. The wedding day is the beginning of a long journey that is full of joy, some negative and positive surprises, some crying, and a lot of training.

Couples spend plenty of money preparing for the wedding day, but they invest nothing in their training so that they can be better husbands and wives. Many do all those vows on the wedding day and yet they are not prepared at all for the big journey that they are starting. Both partners should be born again and filled by the Holy Spirit, teachings only about marriage without the power of God working in the couple cannot do the secret of transforming the couple. The word of God says the two must become one flesh, this cannot happen without the spirit of God, it is a supernatural transaction. The Holy Spirit makes marriage workable. Forgiveness, love, gentleness, goodness, longsuffering, patience, submission are the products of the Holy Spirit. These are the virtues of marriage without which marriage is unbearable, God is key and the center of marriage. Building marriage on some other things ignoring God frustrates and upsets everything.

The two married individuals should have the true love of Jesus in them, and the love of Jesus Christ will cause them to love each other in turn. A person without Christ cannot genuinely love another person. The love of a natural man changes with time and can be affected by situations, and some happenings. In marriage, we need the unchangeable love of Jesus Christ. Mark 12:31 *And the second is like namely this, thou shalt love thy neighbor as thyself. There is no other commandments higher than these.*

Genuine forgiveness is the work of the Holy Spirit, without Him it is impossible to forgive. Forgiveness is a spiritual thing that cannot be done by a mere human being. Divorces are happening because people fail to forgive one another genuinely. There are so many problems fights in the world because people fail to forgive each other, nations fail to forgive other nations that is why there are wars. In a marriage of people not born again, genuine forgiveness is very hard or rather an impossible thing to happen. A husband and wife who has the true love of Jesus Christ in them can love each other more, their individual relationships with God enriches their marriage. They cannot afford to cheat on each other because their individual relationships with God have taught them how to genuinely love. As they are faithful to God, they will be faithful to each other. The stronger the relationship between each spouse with God the stronger their relationship with each other. Natural love between the couple cannot overcome temptations and every marriage relationship goes through so many temptations.

There is a lot of extra-marital affairs going on in many marriages, this is because couples do not have a genuine love for each other which is found in God. When one has the love of God, he or she does not want to do something to someone which he or she does not want to be done to him or her. The love of God teaches and enables spouses to value each other genuinely. A husband or wife without the love of God can view his or her spouse just as a sex object, and if one values his or her partner that way it is easy to engage in extramarital affairs. Marriage was not started by people, it was started by God, therefore born-again people should have better marriages because they know God. As I am talking about being born-again people, I am not talking of people who just go to church. There are so many people who profess to be born again and yet they know nothing about God, they have no relationship at all with God and they do not live according to the word of God, and they do not have the genuine fear of God in them - they are also engaging themselves in divorces.

5

Love is key in marriage

Marriage without God is very difficult because the husband must learn to love his wife from God, who is love. No human being has got genuine love, it is only the love of God that does not fail. The love of man fails when it faces challenges and trials. Human love can only operate in certain conditions, if the conditions change it cannot stand and human love can only operate in certain favourable conditions consequently, we get many divorces in the world. Many times, when men say they love someone what they are actually saying is that they are lustfully being attracted to that person, the love is based on the stature of the person, this is not genuine love but to them, they think it is genuine. It has more to do with the appearance of the person than the personality of the person. Love is a spiritual thing that we can only get from God. Marriage based on human love only cannot stand the pressures and tests that all marriages go through. Marriage is like a long journey that passes through so many valleys, deserts, mountains, and jungles, it goes through many wars, it is tried and tested.

Human love is self-centred, it is concerned with self, and this is the number one reason why it cannot work. Marriage needs the love of God which is concerned with the welfare of the other person. Genuine love thinks of the other person and this is the most important thing that is needed in marriage, think first of your spouse in everything that you do before you consider yourself. God was concerned with the welfare of humanity that is why he was ready to give His only begotten son into the world to save them. Jesus humbled himself to become a man to redeem humanity. God so loved the world that he gave his only begotten son. Genuine love gives. Love is ready to let it go for the benefit of the other person. John 3:16 *For God so loved the world, that he gave his only begotten son, that whosoever believeth in him should not perish, but have everlasting life.* Many get married to be served and not to serve, the husband is looking forward to being served by his wife and the wife is expecting to be served by the husband. We should be getting married to serve each other. Both get into marriage expecting to be served and when this does not happen war begins. Marriage is all about serving someone, Jesus did not come to be served but he came to serve. Greatness and fulfilment in life are found when we serve and not when we get served, Christ had to wash the feet of the disciples. Genuine love is all about giving it away. You cannot say you love until you give it away.

Genuine love is all about making someone better, taking someone from one point to the next. The love of God promotes, and uplifts, Christ came to uplift us up from one point to the next and we are moving from glory to glory. This is the pillar of marriage uplifting each other on daily basis, this cannot be achieved without God, this can only be done by a regenerated born-again man or woman. 1 Corinthians 13:4 -8 *Charity(love) suffereth long, and is kind; charity envieth not; charity vaunteth not itself, is not puffed up, Doth not behave itself unseemingly, seeketh not her own, is not easily provoked, thinking no evil; Rejoiceth not in iniquity, but rejoiceth in the truth; Beareth all things, believeth all things, hopeth all things, endureth all things. Charity never faileth.* The things that are narrated in the above verses are the major causes of divorces. Couples do not have long-suffering to each other, this is a major concern. If the other person cannot do things my way, we should part ways as soon as possible, we are not compatible. They rather live together not married but as partners not committed to each other, so that they can quickly part ways and quietly the moment they discover the other one cannot do things my way. There is no virtue of long-suffering at all, go your way and I go my way. There is no endurance at all, no patience, no sacrifice. Marriage teaches us endurance long-suffering and sacrifice.

The world is chaotic because people think they can live in it anyhow. That is impossible because the one who made it put laws that govern it, if you choose to go against those laws there are judgements that will consequently deal with you whether you like it or not. You cannot ignore the laws of God and get away with it, no, the judgements will always catch up with you in one way or another. Every institution in the world has laws that govern it, and marriage is one of them. Learn the laws and how they operate if you want to enjoy life. If we try to create our own laws and do things the way we choose, we will always suffer. This is what is already happening in the world today, people who go through a divorce go through hell. After going through a divorce, you find the person is destabilised and is full of guilt, hatred and bitterness. Even if one gets into another marriage that new marriage is always being disturbed by some residue from the previous relationship especially if there are children and properties involved. Long-suffering can stop all the pain that people go through after divorce. Many times, the second or third marriages are even worse than the first, why, the person did not learn what he did wrong in the first marriage. The person carries the same problem into the next marriage and the cycle continues.

Kindness is needed most in marriage than anywhere else in the world. Many times, people can be very kind at work, school etc but find it very hard to be kind to their spouses. Every man is kind to a certain extent but when challenged we lose the kindness; we need the kindness of Jesus Christ that has been tried and tested. It is only the kindness of Christ that can overcome, this is what I need in my marriage. My relationship with Christ is of paramount importance because it regulates my relationship with my spouse. When Christ is in me, he restrains me in times when I want to react according to my flesh. Every man by nature is rough, I need Christ to harness me. This is an issue that I always come across in my counselling sessions with spouses complaining that spouses are not kind to each other. The love of God is pure but the love of man is full of jealousy and its possessive. I have seen married people being jealous of each other, fighting bitterly, even going to the extent of killing one another. This is what always happens with the so-called love, which is not genuine that many times those who thought were in love end up being number one enemies. Many things in this world have two sides, the genuine and the fake. Marriage based on human love is fake, it is costly, and it can be very painful. If what I am saying is not true why are people divorcing, they are divorcing because of these things. They deceive each other with fake love and after a few days after spending so much money preparing for a wedding they divorce and all that they thought was love turns into hundred percent enmity. Fake love is like a time bomb.

Human love is arrogant, and there is no marriage that can be built on the spirit of arrogancy. The love of God is not arrogant. People are getting into marriage but full of the spirit of arrogancy, this is the spirit that is controlling the whole world today. People are getting into marriage but already with an exit plan, husband and wife are arrogant they cannot submit to each other. Each one is very much conscious of his rights, and without submission to one another everything goes wrong. The love of God uplifts the life of another person, but the spirit of arrogance is concerned about itself, how can two arrogant people live together? That is the same spirit that caused the devil to be thrown out of heaven, it is only submissive people who can live together. We only get a submissive spirit from Christ, and an arrogant spirit is from the devil. Human rights are given by human beings and everything that is human without God gives problems. Marriages are not meant to be run according to human rights; they are run according to the word of God.

These rights are satanic and are coming from the pit of hell. Submission is seen as weakness and stupidity, yet life is all about submitting one to another. No car can move if the different parts do not submit to each other, submission and unity is power. The parts of the car must first be united and submit to each other for the car to move, the moment one part does not submit the car cannot move.

True human rights are enshrined in the word of God, God created man and He knows what is best for him to live profitably. Human rights should not be taught by people who are clueless about God and do not have any relationship with Him. Man did not come into existence by chance, but he was created by God for a purpose. When God made him, He made laws by which he is supposed to live by. Marriage operates according to the word of God not according to human rights which are man-made. Marriage is based on divine principles of God, anything that is man-made has consequences and problems. Marriage is spiritual and must be lived thus. Human beings are spiritual, therefore everything about their lives is spiritual. The true love of God is not boastful or vainglorious. Without the knowledge of God, every natural man is boastful of his achievements. Spouses compete, each feels he has done so much in the relationship and the other is just benefitting. The same spirit of arrogance brings all these things and many marriages have come to a halt. Genuine Love wants to see the other person benefitting even more. The love of God is concerned with the well-being of the other person.

Love is not haughty, haughty people are arrogant, proud, hot-headed, they see themselves better than others and feel superior to others. They feel they know it all, do not take any advice or correction from any-one. Now imagine having two such people living together as husband and wife, what is the obvious thing that will happen. According to my assessment, these are the kind of people that communities are produc-ing, if we go into many schools, homes, , nations we find these are the characteristics of the people that are being produced. When they get married, they cannot last long in that marriage because of the way they were brought up. They are being brought up in communities where selfishness, arrogance are the normal trends.

Today's people do not want to follow regulations, they think to be free is to do what I feel like doing. There is nowhere in the world where you can do what you want to do, you must follow certain channels and rules if you want to be free. Freedom is the ability to be able to live according to laws that govern any institute in which you find yourself in.

The love of God does not insist on its own rights or its own way. Naturally, every man wants and insists on things to be done their own way. Marriage becomes impossible if each one involved wants things to be done their own way. The two people need to learn to surrender and to submit to each other. Even if I want things to happen my own way I must learn to let go and follow what the other person wants to be done. Submitting to another person is not a sign of weakness, it is in fact wisdom and strength, fools are the ones who cannot submit. Therefore, many women do not want to submit to their husbands as the bible says, they think if they do that it means they are second class inferior people, which is not correct at all. A person without the love of God is self-seeking and self-centred. He will only do those things that benefit him or her. When people are looking for someone to get married to, these are things to check in the life of that person but unfortunately, people just want the physical appearance of the person. A person is not his or her physical appearance, the real person is hidden inside the body. Physical appearance can mislead you and many have been misled.

Today many people hide behind makeup and their nice suits. People are mesmerised by the makeup and the suits and they think they have found the right person to marry but only to discover a few days later in the marriage that they are married to someone far much different from the person they thought that person was. You need the Holy Spirit to help you find the right person to marry. The Holy Spirit must help you see the spiritual person that is hidden in that make-up and the suit. You need revelation by the Holy Spirit, if the Holy Spirit is not involved in your dating, you might think you know the person you want to get married to and yet you know nothing about that person. You are only seeing the physical, but the spiritual part is hidden from you until you start to live together. People still divorce yet they spent five years dating. During dating, you do not see reality because your eyes are so much covered with lust which most people think is love.

Love is not a feeling, genuine love is only found in God, He is love. Christ is the love of God manifest, therefore, without Christ, no one can have genuine love, Love is spiritual. It is not easily provoked or angered. If there was no provocation in marriage, there would be no divorces. Couples provoke one another easily and on daily basis. All verbal wars that take place in families is a result of anger. Therefore, I say it is very important for spouses to have a relationship with Christ. The two people should be born again. A person who is born of God has the spirit of God reigning in his life. The same spirit can teach him to control his temper and anger. Marriages are coming to a halt because of anger issues. Fights break out because of bouts of uncontrollable anger. Forbearance, love bears all things, it endures all things. If there is anything that is needed in marriage it's endurance, without endurance all things fail. As I said earlier, marriage is like a journey that takes you through mountains, valleys, and jungles you need to endure to the end. When people get married the marriage is tried and tested from all angles. The marriage responsibilities weigh you down, you need to endure and the capacity to endure comes from God. A natural man can endure for some time, but he will give up. It is the endurance that we get from God that can get us to the end. The love of God does not fail us, this is what we need in marriage. How many people had all the confidence in the love of their spouses but only to discover that the spouse was cheating on them? That is human love it will always fail us. If you want a shipwreck in your life believe in human love, people change but God does not change. People can say they love you today but tomorrow the same will dump you, I have seen this happening several times.

Christ is love that is why he continues to love us although we do not live up to his expectation, His love endures for ever. 1John 4:7-8 *Beloved, let us love one another: for love is of God; and everyone that loveth is born of God, and knoweth God. He that loveth not knoweth not God; for God is love.* His love for us is not conditioned by what we do to him. It is always there for us whether we do good or wrong, whether we appreciate his love or not he is still the same, the love is not changed by what I do, even not by my attitude towards him. Hebrews 13:8 *Jesus Christ the same yesterday, and today, and forever.*

6

Independence and submission

Romans 7:2 *For the woman which hath an husband is bound by the law to her husband so long as he liveth; but if the husband be dead, she is loosed from the law of her husband.* If one insists to be independent, then they should not get married. Marriage is a covenant that binds two people together and they start to live for one another. The bible says they become one flesh and marriage is dependent on your spouse. This is a major cause of divorces because people want to live independently. Marriage is putting the interests of your spouse first before yours. Before I do something, I must consider how what I want to do will affect my spouse.

Ephesians 5:22 *Wives, submit yourselves unto your own husbands, as unto the Lord.* Submission is dependence and it has been misunderstood by many. When you submit to someone you are not subhuman, and you are not weak. When I submit, I am not under oppression or suppression and I am not inferior to the person that I submit to. Life is built on submission and without it life is impossible. The world has become chaotic because of this simple reason. Christ submitted to His Father, but he was not inferior to him. Jesus Christ and the Father God are one, when he submitted to his father, he was not being suppressed nor was he oppressed. John 10:30 I and my Father are one. Then the Jews took up stones again to stone him. God the Father, God the Son, and God the Holy Spirit submit to one another that is how they are three in one. If Christ had refused to submit to his father, he could not have come to redeem humanity. The plan of God to redeem the world was made possible because of submission.

Submission is spiritual, we can only learn it from Christ. Therefore, a marriage without Christ can prove to be very difficult because there is nowhere the couple can learn submission. Both husband and wife must learn to submit, from Christ. If they cannot submit to Christ, they are not able to submit to one another. What happens in marriage is determined by the relationship that is there between each spouse and Jesus. The bible says *women submit to your own husbands*. Ephesians 5:24 *Therefore as the church is subject unto Christ, so let the wives be to their own husbands in everything.* Many women do not like this verse they wish it was not in the bible because they have a wrong concept about it. Men on the other hand wish this verse was repeated several times in the bible, they also have a wrong concept. Men think that they have been given a mandate by God to treat women as second-class citizens. Everyone must submit to someone if ever there is going to be order and peace in every institution.

We must submit to one another in the fear of God in marriage. In some cultures and religions, they use the above verse to oppress and suppress women. Men in such religions and cultures think that they are superior to women. In such circles women are considered useless, they cannot think, they are not smart, they cannot make sound decisions, they are only good for sex . The bible also says that the husband is head of the wife, they think that it is another mandate from God to ill-treat their wives. John 5:23 *For the husband is the head of the wife, even as Christ is the head of the church; and he is saviour of the body.* They believe God gave them authority to dominate and do whatever they see fit to their women. This is all the rubbish of the devil. Christ is the head of the church; we must learn from him. The church is the bride of Christ, we must see how he treats his bride. He does not dominate over the church, but he loves her, he protects her, he is busy perfecting her and he even died for her. Christ is loved by the bride because of the great love that he has shown towards her. He does not super impose himself upon her - he has long-suffering towards her full of mercy and patience towards her.

True headship is taking care of the people that you are leading. Christ leads her bride by serving her, he is servant to her bride. Ephesians 5:25 *Husbands, love your wives, even as Christ loved the church, and gave himself for it; That he might sanctify and cleanse it with the washing of water by the word, That he might present it to himself a glorious church, not having spot, or wrinkle, or any such thing; but that it should be holy and without blemish. So ought men to love their wives as their own bodies. He that loveth his wife loveth himself. For no man ever yet hated his own flesh; but nourisheth it, even as the Lord the church:* The position of headship is earned by serving. The husband is the head but if he has no ability to serve, he cannot lead. Leadership is giving service to the people that you lead. Christ came to serve and not to be served. Matthew 20: 23 *"But it shall be so among you: but whosoever will be great among you, let him be your minister; And whosoever will be chief among you, let him be your servant: Even as the son of man came not to be ministered unto, but to minister, and to give his life a ransom for many."* Every husband has been called to serve his wife first and foremost. Unfortunately, the opposite is happening therefore we are witnessing the chaotic situation that we are having in marriages globally- men demand to be served.

Christ is fundamental in marriage, a husband without Christ has got nowhere he can learn to love and to lead. There is a big problem in the world many people who hold positions of authority think they are there to be served. Every public office that you find yourself in you are there to serve and not to be served. Many leaders do not understand that they are servants and not bosses. We learn true leadership from Jesus Christ.

Institutions are suffering all over the world because people who are in leadership do not understand what leadership is all about. They are bosses they do not accept any corrections or criticism; they know it all. There is a great shortage of true leadership in the world. We have dictator husbands in many homes, running the affairs of their families with an iron rod. Husband, you are the head of the family, your duty is to improve the lives of the people that you are heading. Professor Ezekiel Guti in his book, A Wise man on pages 69 -70 says " The husband should be the protector; God is the husband to creation just as Jesus is the bridegroom and the church is the bride. So, man ought to care for the wife just as God does to his people. God protected the children of Israel against the enemy and fought the wars for them. Joshua 11:6 But the Lord said to Joshua do not be afraid because of them."

Jesus Christ is both King and servant, he is our king, but he came to serve us - the husband is also both king and servant. My school of thought says headship once given it must be earned through servanthood. God has given the husband a position as head of his wife, but he must earn it by serving. Let your wife put you into that position that God has given you by the service that you offer to her. If she does not put you in that position, then you are irrelevant in everything that you do in that marriage. Husband be a lover, not an imposter and love triggers submission from the wife. If we only knew this great truth that we learn from our Lord Jesus Christ, the world would be a better place to live and marriage would be enjoyable. All leadership positions whether political, church, social, if people only understood that leadership is all about serving people would not be fighting for leadership positions. Today leadership positions mean, fame, money, power etc, they are fighting to get into the positions for these reasons. It is not true that they are getting into those positions to serve. True leadership is sacrificing your life for others like what our Lord Jesus Christ did. The husband must be there for his wife, must be ready to die for her. When this kind of headship is shown it will voluntarily unleash submission from the wife.

Jesus is our king because of what he did for us, submission is unleashed automatically in us when we come to understand the great work that he did at Calvary and what he is still doing in our lives.

Life is impossible without submission. Ephesians 5:20-21 *Giving thanks always for all things unto God and the Father in the name of our Lord Jesus Christ; Submitting yourselves one to another in the fear of God.* Submission is not only necessary in a marriage but in all sectors of life. Principles must submit to another for them to cause things to function. You must submit to your friend to keep your friendship going. The moment you stop submitting to each other that is the end of the friendship. As you submit to one another you are not inferior to him and he is not inferior to you. You submit to your boss at work, but it does not mean that you are not a human being. Your body parts must submit to each other for you to be able to live when they do not you die. If there is no submission in marriage that marriage shuts down and it dies.

Submission a response to love

1 Corinthians 11:3 *But I would have you know that the head of every man is Christ; and the head of the woman is the man; and the head of Christ is God.*

Ephesians 5;22,25 *Wives , submit yourselves unto your own husbands, even as Christ also loved the church, and gave himself for it.*

Submission is a response to love, and it cannot be demanded. It is not only women who should submit, men must submit to Christ and Christ to God. The husband must submit to Christ for him to tap and learn love from him. He must transmit that love to his wife and the wife will respond by submitting to him. Wives have not been asked to love their husbands by God. Their responsibility is to submit to their husbands. It is the man who must love his wife so that in turn he gets the submission. Submission and love make marriage complete. These two things make husband and wife one. Love is found in Christ and submission is found in Christ. No man without Christ can love neither is there any woman without Christ who can submit. I am talking of the genuine permanent love of God not the love of people. The love of people is the one that has caused all the divorces. Outside Christ people do not have genuine love. The love of people can change, it can be affected by many factors, but the love of Jesus does not change forever. When a woman is loved with the genuine love of God, she will automatically surrender her will and do the will of her husband. If men can love the way Christ loves the church this is what happens the woman will surrender everything to her husband.

Christ loves us so much and that is why Paul says it's no longer him living but Christ. Galatians 2:20 *I am crucified with Christ: nevertheless, I live; not I, but Christ liveth in me: and the life which I now live in the flesh I live by faith of the son of God, who loved me and gave himself for me.* Paul surrendered everything so much that he ceased to live but had to let Christ live instead. John also says let him decrease but Christ increase. John 3:30 *He must increase, but I must decrease.* A woman is wired to submit to Christ her creator therefore if she sees something that is not of Christ in the man it is very hard for her to submit. She has been made to submit to the love of Christ only if she sees anything else rebellion is unleashed from her. Some men want their wives to submit to them, but they do not want to submit to Christ. Going to church or just being a member of a certain church cannot make one submissive to Christ. We have many people who go to church but are not submissive to Christ.

Many people when they want to get married, go to church, thinking they will get the best wife or husband. It is not about just going to church it is about the relationship that that person has with Christ. Many after marrying a church person they get heartbroken because they thought people who go to church are the best. Being submissive to Christ is another thing different from just going to church. We learn submission best from no other person except Christ. Christ lived in total submission to the father ever, he lived the will of the Father, not his. John 6:38 *"For I came down from heaven, not to do mine own will, but the will of him that sent me". He did what he saw his Father doing not what he wanted.* John 5: 19 *" Then answered Jesus and said unto them, verily verily, I say unto you, the Son can do nothing of himself, but what he seeth the Father do: for what things soever he doeth, these also doeth the Son likewise". He said what the Father said not what he wanted to say, lived to fulfill the will of the Father. He obeyed the Father even unto death.* John 2:8 *"And being found in fashion as a man, he humbled himself, and became obedient unto death, even the death of the cross."*

Submission is not easy, as I said earlier own that it is spiritual and divine no natural man can do it. You need the power of the Holy Spirit in you who is the spirit of submission – it is imparted to you by the Holy Spirit. John1:8 *" But ye shall receive power, after that the Holy Ghost is come upon you : and ye shall be witnesses unto me both in Jerusalem, and unto the uttermost part of the earth." Christ is fundamental in marriage; it must be built upon Christ who is the sure foundation the rock.* Matthew 7:24 -25 *"Therefore whosoever heareth these sayings of mine, and doeth them, I will liken him unto a wise man, which built his house upon a rock: And when the rain descended, and the floods came, and the winds blew, and beat upon the house; and it fell not: for it was founded upon a rock."* These two things love, and submission cannot be done by the strength of a human being, it can only be done by the spirit of God. I have heard people saying give flowers to your wife to show that you love her. Flowers can only help the fake love, human love. We get love from God who is living not from a flower that is dead. A flower does not know whether it is alive or not therefore there is no way it can enhance love.

If this is correct that flowers add love, we should not be having so many divorces because on Valentine's day many shops run out of flowers. Check on this one if you forget to buy flowers for your wife when she is expecting some from you what happens, she may get angry and this can grow into a very big issue that might even add up to a divorce. It is good to buy flowers and gifts, but the secret is in God. I witnessed a couple that went through a divorce because of these flowers. I tried to help them, but the issue had grown so big that they divorced.

Divine Authority

A person who is not under authority cannot have authority because authority is conferred upon someone by those who are in authority already. God oversees the husband, the wife, and children, therefore God must give the husband authority to lead the family. A man who is not born again is not living under the authority of God. A person who is under authority does not do what he wants but he does what he is directed to do by those who are above him. Marriage is an institution of God and husbands as heads of that institution must be under his authority for the safety of those that he is leading. He must lead them according to the laws of God not his own laws. A man who is not under the authority of Jesus Christ is the most dangerous person to live with, he is more dangerous than an animal. Such a person is very unpredictable and can do anything at any time because he is not accountable to anyone. All husbands must be accountable to Christ for how they run their families.

Families in the world are in trouble because they are being led by people who are rebellious against the authority of God. Children are rebelling against their parents because they learned rebellion from their fathers who are rebelling against their Father God. Children are not accepting the authority of their fathers because their authority is not from God and it is the same with wives. The husbands are superimposing their authority upon them. The husbands have never learned to be in authority from God. The world has gone wild, it all started with the fathers who have forsaken the authority of God upon their lives. Malachi 3:7 *Even from the days of your Fathers ye are gone away from mine ordinances, and have not kept them. Return unto me, and I will return unto you, saith the Lord of hosts. But ye said, Wherein shall we retain?* Husbands, we share the same name with the God of heaven, which means we must learn from him to be true husbands and fathers. We are not husbands and fathers just because we have the seed and we are able to impregnate someone. We are fathers because we can lead those whom we have brought into the world. We do not do that by just feeding them and clothing them, we should show them where we came from, we should point them to God and they should meet with the living God.

Men, we are responsible for many of the bad things that are happening in the world today. All the wars that are happening are caused mainly by men, children and women are suffering as a result, yet we are supposed to be protecting them. Prostitution that is happening in the world is being fuelled by men if they stopped it, it would stop. Men are refusing to live under the authority of God chaos is rampant in the world. You are now safe in the jungle with animals than to be in the best cities of the world with men. How many children are in the world who are fatherless, yet their fathers are not dead? We learn to submit to authority when we come to Christ because Christ is submission. When Christ comes into our lives, we receive the spirit of submission and we understand authority. A man who does not have Christ in him has the spirit of the devil and of the world. The devil rebelled against God and wanted his throne to be higher than the throne of God. A person who is not born again is generally rebellious and does not understand authority. The devil hates authority, therefore, he tried to usurp power from God. Isaiah 14:13 *For thou hast said in thine heart, I will ascend into heaven, I will exalt my throne above the stars of God: I will sit also upon the mount of the congregation, in the sides of the north:* It is very dangerous to get involved in a marriage with someone who is not born again. He or she is not bound by any laws and is rebellious by nature - does not recognize neither does he or she have any respect of authority and does not understand covenants. Marriage is a covenant, and that covenant can only be respected by someone who is already in covenant with Christ. People who are not born again are controlled by emotions and the environment where they are. They do not believe that God exists therefore they can break the marriage covenant at any time as their emotions and feelings lead them. If they see someone who looks better than their own spouse, they do not feel guilty leaving their current spouse and going for the next one. They are led and controlled by their feelings and emotions.

There is a very narrow chance for spouses who fear God to divorce I do not mean those who just go to church but do not have the fear of God. Without the practical living knowledge of God, no human being has the full understanding of the value of another man. You do not fully understand who human beings are unless you have God in your life. The more we understand who God is the more we start to understand who human beings are. A spouse who does not know God does not really understand who his or her spouse is. If you understand human beings from God's point of view you cannot ill-treat another person. You cannot think of divorce because you understand the pain that another person is going to go through, and you would not want them to go through that. A person without God does not care what other people go through. They enjoy it when someone is suffering. A human being is not a toy that you can choose to do whatever you want to do with.

This is the biggest problem that many marriages are going through in the world. Spouses live together but they have absolutely no idea of the value of the person that they are living with. People are ignorant of what they are worth. We learn of our worth and of others when we understand who God is and our relationship with him. If people continue to think that they evolved from a chimpanzee then they will continue to act like a chimpanzee. If you do not understand where you came from then you cannot understand what you are worth. Many people have believed the lies that they evolved from animals and that is why they are behaving like animals. If you understand that you were made in the image of God and that you came out of God, you will behave like a god. . Genesis 1:26 *"And God said, let us make man in our image, after our likeness: and let them have dominion over the fish of the sea, and over the fowl of the air, and over the cattle, and over all the earth, and over every creeping thing that creepeth upon the earth."* People behave like animals, they have got no feelings towards each other, therefore, spouses are divorcing without feeling guilty. Children go through traumatic times when parents divorce, but the parents have no feelings towards the children even towards each other. It is now fashionable to be in a second third fourth marriage. It is also fashionable to be living with a stepmother, stepfather, stepsister, stepbrother, etc.

Every human being is wired to be accountable to God, therefore when you do something wrong you feel guilty. Even if you try to ignore you feel things are not okay with you, it is because you are made to be accountable. It is only God who teaches a human being to be accountable. When you love God, you cannot lie because you know you must be accountable. You cannot even lie to your spouse because you know you are accountable to God. You cannot afford to cheat your spouse because you are accountable to God. Spouses who are not accountable to God find it very hard to do bad things to their spouses. They cannot lie, cheat, mistreat their loved ones because they are accountable to God. Your spouse cannot be accountable to you if they are not accountable to God first. We learn to be accountable to each other as we relate to God. If a person has no relationship with God, you cannot rely on him or her and he cannot be accountable to you. Lying and cheating are the major causes of divorces, spouses are not honest with one another. It's only God who can teach us to be honest with each other. Women want security in marriage. The security they need is not mainly money or properties, they need assurance from the husband that they are the only ones being loved. That is very important to them. They are not much interested in money and all these material things from their men. What they need most is love and that is why even poor people get married if they can convince a woman beyond doubt, that they love her. Ladies need love more than the material things that men may offer. God created them to be loved and they accept love wholeheartedly unlike men. Love means a lot to a woman than to a man. When men talk of love many times, they mean sex, they cannot separate love from sex.

Without Christ, it is hard to provide this kind of security because you will be found wanting as you continue to live together. She will find out and discover your lies, once that happens, she closes and does not trust you again. People change from time to time, but Christ does not change yesterday today and forever. Hebrews 13:8 *"Jesus Christ the same yesterday, and today, and for ever."* Christ is therefore fundamental in marriage. Christ helps you not to be changed by situations and challenges. The church has security in Christ because he does not change. Wives need husbands who are like Christ who do not change or get moved by situations. Where there is no security there is no submission, security gives birth to submission from the wife.

9

Headship - greater responsibility

When you are asked to lead an institution, it means more is expected from you. The higher the position the bigger the responsibility. When God said that the husband is the head of the wife it means more is expected from the husband than from the wife. Many people like positions but they do not want the responsibilities that go with them. Mostly those who love positions are ignorant of the responsibilities that go with the positions. Responsible people do not fight for positions. Many husbands when they hear that they are the head of the wife rejoice because they are not aware of what is expected of them. In their minds, they have wrong concepts of what it means to be the head. When we get into marriage men should discard the boyish mentality and become real men. Boys do not have the fiber to lead families. Unfortunately, we have many boys running families. One of the characteristics of boys is that they run away when things get tough. Professor Ezekiel Guti in his book A Wise Man, Introduction says, " The great cry of women for their husbands is to be real husbands and real fathers to the children have led me to the writing of this book. This points out the need for a crying wife and child for a fulfilling husband and father. When a woman leaves her father and mother to be a wife to someone not born in her family and changes her surname for her husband's that shows total commitment, full trust, and love." There is a big cry out there for real husbands, with the capacity to lead.

Men can only become real husbands by learning from Jesus Christ who is the best husband and leader. Christ is the bridegroom and the church his bride. As head of the wife and of the family what is expected from us? Men we are expected to love, that is our number one job. Whatever we do as we lead; we must do it with love. Provide for the family, my wife is only my helper she must help me provide for the family. The husband must lead his wife and children by example in everything. What I want my wife and children to do, I must do it first. As the leader of the family, I am saying follow me. Christ came to show us the way to do things. He did not tell us to do things that he did not do. He demonstrated everything that he tells us to do. As a husband, I must guide my family. How do I guide it if I do not know what I am doing? To be able to guide my family I must be guided by the spirit of God. I need to be a student every day of my life learning from the leader Jesus Christ otherwise I will derail the whole plan of God about my family. The family is not a property for the husband, it belongs to God. The husband is only a steward or custodian, if only a custodian it means he must always hear from the owner concerning how best he can guide and lead.

The husband is the watchman of the family. He must protect it feeding it with the word of God and without the word of God, the family will disintegrate. The word of God gives wisdom to the members of the family on how to operate in the world. The husband is a priest or shepherd of the family and must point his family to God. Unfortunately, today, most husbands are clueless about their duties. They are good at scattering their seed and impregnating every woman that opens her legs to them and after that do not take any responsibility to look after the child and its mother. The world is becoming chaotic every day because most men are not responsible. Men we need to take away the boyish mentality and be real men. Civilization cannot train us to be better fathers and husbands nor can science do that. Divorces are happening and affecting civilized people and uncivilized alike, the educated and the uneducated. This proves that we need to turn to Christ for us to learn how to live as families. Science and civilization did not make man, but he was made by God, therefore God knows better what is best for man.

10

Wife as a helper

God created a woman with a very big capacity to help. She has that capacity because that is the purpose why she was created in the first place. She has the capacity to help a man to succeed or to fail in life. This depends on how a man handles her. She can be a very dangerous weapon if she is treated without wisdom. Eve helped Adam and humanity to fail. Adam did not know how to handle her, he left her to do things on her own without him checking on what she was doing as her leader. I do not think that when she met with the snake it was the first day. I think she was doing this many days just going out alone without Adam. The serpent should have been seeing her for some days alone roaming the garden, until one day the serpent approached her and engaged her into a conversation. Always check what your wife is doing do not leave her on her own, she may do things that may put the whole family in trouble.

The husband ought to live with her wife according to knowledge and understanding from God. She is wired to respond to the moves and leadership of the husband. If she does not get the leadership from her husband problems start. If you love her, she will respond by submission. If she is not loved she multiplies what you are giving her and gives it back to you. Give her bitterness she will multiply that bitterness and give it back to you. Try to scold her she will give it back to you multi-plied. She gives back to you what you give her, give her joy she will give it back to you. She works in sync with what you give her, she is made that way by God. Since she has the capacity to give back what you give to her, she becomes the reflection of her husband. The church cannot give to Christ what he has not given her. The praise and the love that the church gives back to Christ she gets that from him therefore, the church is the reflection of Christ. When we look at the church, we can see Christ, his goodness, mercy and love. When we look at a wife, we can see the type of her husband that she has. Proverbs 12:4 *A virtuous woman is a crown to her husband:but she that maketh ashamed is as rottenness in his bones.*

11

The cry for mummy's breast

This is a serious stage that needs to be handled with wisdom and knowledge in marriage. This usually happens when the first-born child arrives. Many divorces do happen usually when couples have one or two children. When the first child comes normally the wife is overwhelmed by a sudden load of responsibilities. The arrival of the new baby ushers in so many demands and responsibilities to the poor mother who many times is not ready to shoulder those responsibilities. The child wants the presence of the mother twenty-four seven. The husband wants his wife twenty-four seven and day to day house chores. It becomes too much for her and if she is employed her job wants her 24/7 -too, many demands upon one person.

What usually happens is when the child comes the wife unconsciously shifts her attention from the husband to the child and she becomes fully occupied with the child. Taking care of the child takes away her attention from the husband. She finds it very hard to share her love with the two, the child and the husband. Before the child came, she had all her attention towards her husband. When the child comes, the husband misses the attention that he used to enjoy. Usually, he suffers silently . The husband feels deserted, lonely, and unwanted because the wife is now busy with the baby. The baby and the husband start to fight silently for the attention of one person. The husband used to enjoy the breasts of her wife without anyone disturbing him, now he must share those breasts with the baby.

Usually, the husband is missing them the most because they are being given to the child. The man if not trained will get frustrated. There is a silent war between the child and the father. Sometimes as the couple is trying to have sex the child starts screaming everything must stop, mum has to attend to the baby, disturbance after disturbance. This can be very frustrating on the part of the husband. Husband and wife may start some quarrels because of this. Instead of embracing or cuddling in bed with his wife, the wife is cuddling with the baby. This season can be dangerous if couples are not prepared for it and this is the time when extramarital relationships may start.

The husband should understand the phase, should be able to help her wife so that she may not be overwhelmed with what she will be going through. The wife also needs to understand her husband she must try not to make him feel abandoned. The child is after the breast the father is after the same breast. The two guys are obsessed with it. Share it fairly mum otherwise, disaster will strike the young family!!!!!!!!

12

Training up of children

God gives parents to children to take care of them for him. We must raise them up according to his ways, not our ways because they are not ours, we are just custodians, they belong to him. What happens to them we shall be held accountable. Besides giving them food, clothing, and shelter we must spend time teaching them the ways of God. Teach them who they are and where they came from and where they are going from the word of God. At school, they are taught things that concern this physical world only. Some of the things they are taught are not true for example they are taught that they evolved from a chimpanzee and as a result, they have an identity crisis. They are told things like, the world came into being after a big bung, the evolution theory which is all heresy. It is our biggest responsibility as parents to teach children from the word of God, who they are, where they came from where they are going, and their purpose. Genesis 1:26 28 *And God said, Let us make man in our own image, after our likeness: and let them have dominion over the fish of the sea, and over the fowl of the air, and over every creepin thing that creepeth upon the earth. So God created man in his own image, in the image of God created he him; male and female created he them. And God blessed them, and God said unto them, be fruitful, and multiply, and replenish the earth, and subdue it: and have dominion over the fish of the sea, and over the fowl of the air, and over every living thing that movath upon the earth."*

When a person does not know the purpose why he is living, his life is full of confusion, frustration, and hopelessness. Without purpose, it means the person is ready to engage in anything to try to make that thing a purpose for his living. Taking drags can become a purpose of life for such a person and demons also attack and use people with no purpose. A person who has the following questions not answered in his or her life usually leads a miserable life.

The questions are

1. Who am I?
2. Where did I come from?
3. Where am I going?
4. For what purpose am I living?

Life is centered on these questions. If there are no answers to these questions people will live their lives anyhow. It is the duty of parents to give answers to these questions and explain everything to their children. These questions are not answered at school because the answers to them are only found in the word of God and the bible has been removed from schools. Here comes the biggest problem, many parents do not have answers to these questions themselves, they are also wondering. A parent who does not know God does not have answers to these questions even if he is educated with all the education of the world. The questions can be taught by the Holy Spirit to someone who is born again only. Earlier on in this book, I said the knowledge of God is fundamental for us to have better and more successful marriages. In the first formative years of a child from zero to about 15years of age, a child is hundred percent connected to the parents and the parents are everything to him. He believes in the parents and takes in everything they teach him or her. During this window period, parents must lay a strong foundation through the word of God in the life of the child. This window is not open forever. Things will change usually when the child comes to about 15 years of age and over. Parents we are the first teachers of our children. It is the foundation that we lay in these formative years that must guide the life of the child into adulthood. Proverbs 22:6 *"Train up a child in the way he should go: and when he is old, he will not depart from it."* Proverbs 1:8-11 *"My son hear the instruction of thy father and forsake not the law of thy mother: For they shall be an ornament of grace unto thy head, and chains about thy neck. My son, if sinners entice thee, consent thou not. If they say, come with us, let us lay wait for blood, let us lurk privily for the innocent without cause."*

Children cannot understand as they grow that which is acceptable to God and that which is not acceptable unless they are taught by the parents. We should not allow our children to be taught by people whom we do not know. However, this is what is happening today. We send our children to schools, but we do not know the lives of the teachers that are teaching our children. They are in the hands of those teachers throughout the week every day. We just take the children in the evening to sleep at home but the following morning they are in the hands of that teacher whom we do not know. When a child gets into their teens everything normally changes about them. His trust and confidence are shifted to friends and other people. They start to see their parents as people who are irrelevant, backward, ignorant of what life is, he feels he has a better understanding of how to handle things and issues better than his parents. He wants to go far away from his parents and live alone because he feels his parents are disturbing his freedom. He puts his trust in friends, teachers, other people, television personalities, social media, books, celebrities, etc. There are so many changes taking place in his or her body that produces different kinds of pressures which makes him or her think that he is old enough to make independent decisions. These biological and spiritual pressures continue to mount up until a child gets into young adult age.

If we missed laying a strong foundation through the word of God during the formative years, we will lose the child. He will go wild and many times we cannot bring them back again to become responsible citizens. The word of God is very clear that parents ought to give instruction and understanding to their children. They must give sound doctrine and wisdom to their children. This will keep and protect them from error as they grow. Proverbs 4:1 - *"Hear, ye children, the instruction of a father, and attend to know understanding. For I give you good doctrine, forsake ye not my law. For I was my father's son, tender and only beloved in the sight of my mother. He taught me also, and said unto me, let thine heart retain my words; keep my commandments, and live. Get wisdom, get understanding: forget it not; neither decline from the words of my mouth."*

Many parents are deceived when the child is between zero and fifteen years of age. She or he is like an angel you cannot believe that one day that child can become very wild. When you hear or see other people having hard times with their children you think yours will never do that. If we do not teach our children, the world is busy teaching them every day. As we take our children to school at whatever level they are very busy drilling worldly wisdom into the child. They are busy making him what they want him to be. The schools are busy molding your child into a worldly person. Sooner or later you will know that they were surely working very hard with those teachers when you start to hear your child saying some nasty things to you, things that you never thought your child could say to you. Schools ignorantly are teaching our children humanistic teachings full of the influence of demons and we end up having rebellious children that are full spirit of the world that is running the world. Rebellion starts at home, the child rebels against his or her parents. Then it goes into the community, the same child does not respect any authority, from there it goes to his place of work when he starts working, he does not want to work. The person does what he wants to do and does not follow rules and regulations at the workplace. From there it develops into an unruly citizen, the person does not want to follow any instructions, does not even want to respect road signs and speed limits in the road. The devil is building a society that does not respect all authority. His aim is to have a chaotic world. Professor Ezekiel GUTI says in his book; Strategies For Saving Marriages for this generation page 8 "You cannot have a good family if there is no good marriage. There is no way you can have a good community unless you have good families. When there is a problem in marriage, the problem will spread to the family. From the family, it will spread in schools and to the community, from community to the companies, to the towns and cities."

The devil is keeping parents busy with work so that they cannot have time with their children. Children are being raised by the television and the internet. Parents are only providing food, shelter, and clothing for the children no life values are being imparted into the children. Children are getting their values from celebrities whom they watch on television. Many children do not desire to be like their parents because they are not bonded to them. They are connected to the teachers at kindergarten, high school, university, and what they watch on television. Parents have become foreigners to their own children. They are raised by teachers at the kindergarten. The world has been commercialized; many people are only living just to make as much money as they can but at the expense of the lives of their children. Many parents have sold out the lives of their children because of the love of money. They are busy trying to make money which many are still failing to make. They only make enough for rent and food, not good food for that matter but just average food. Many children do not breastfeed enough, a few months down the line the child must be weaned because mum has to go back to work - child abuse. The child has the right to breastfeed, but he is deprived. What do you think this does to the child? The child cannot express it but inside of him, there is a war going on. The child suffers from rejection, the child is going through so much pain which he cannot express at that moment but will be expressed later on in life in many different bad ways. When a child is breastfeeding there is a special bonding going on between the child and the mother and biologically the mother's milk is best for the child's development.

We have got a world of people full of frustration, rejection, and anger. This can be attributed to the things that we have been discussing above. Some of the teachers at the kindergarten are not there because they have children at heart. Some just want to make money that is the primary purpose they are doing the job. Some of them ill-treat our children during our absence. The child cannot explain what he is going through, but he is going through trauma. There are so many abuses going on in some of these institutions which people do not know which the child is going through but are unable to narrate. I have discovered that some who work in these institutions they are there on a mission of the devil, to put some evil spirits into our children while they are still young. They join the institutions for the sake of destroying the future lives of our children.

The devil is the engineer of all that is going on in the world and has created conditions that force both parents to go to work and leave their children alone. It is now very hard for a family to survive on one salary. On the other hand, he has created greed for money for material things in people so much that they do not care what is going on with their children as long as they are making money. There is so much competition in the world that people lose sleep when they see someone making progress more than themselves. In all this big world race, in the mist and dust of it all, parents lose their children to the devil and they lose themselves to him as well. There is a race!!! King Solomon who tried it all says all is vanity. Ecclesiastes 1:2,8 *"Vanity of vanities; all is vanity. What profit hath a man of all his labour which he taketh under the sun? All things are full of labour; man cannot utter it; the eye is not satisfied with seeing, nor the ear filled with hearing."* It is not the work of the church, Children's Department to train your child for you. Their job is to complement what you are doing as a parent. We should not transfer our responsibility to them.

It is impossible for parents to be able to raise children in the right manner if they do not understand the stages of development of a child from birth to the time he becomes an adult. There must be communication channels put in place for the child to be able to relate with parents. Parents must help the child to learn to behave according to the word of God. The child must know what behavior is expected of him or her. The child should know that they cannot do whatever they want to do but that there are limits, there are certain things that he cannot be done. Some are unknowingly building the lives of their children upon drugs, drunkenness, prostitution, rebelliousness, marijuana, pornography, etc. The children are learning these things from their parents every day in their homes, schools, towns, and cities. We cannot have a better society when those who should set standards for society do not know what they are doing.

If we do not point our children to Christ by how we live they will live to regret their lives when they become adults. Ecclesiastes 12:1 *"Remember your creator in the days of your youth, before the days of trouble come and the years approach when you will say, I find no pleasure in them"* Our children shall not find pleasure in their lives if we do not help them to know their creator who has better plans for them. Jeremiah 29:11 *"For I know the thoughts that I think toward you, saith the Lord, thoughts of peace, and not of evil, to give you an expected end."*

Our children need to be taught by their parents that they should not build their lives upon what they feel in their bodies. They must live upon the word of God. What they feel is not the right thing to do, they need to be trained and helped to control their feelings for example when they come to their teens they start to have sexual feelings. This does not mean that they should start to practice sex. The feelings that they are having are only showing that they are developing in the right manner for them to be able to engage in sexual activities when they get married. Sex is for married people only. Romans 8:13 *"For if ye live after the flesh, ye shall die: but if ye through the Spirit do mortify the deeds of the body, ye shall live."* Children should be helped so that they may become children of God, they must be born again. How can they be born again if the parents are not born again, they are just religious people who do not know God themselves. We cannot have better generations of people without Christ. Our children need to understand the youthful desires that are inherent in them how to deal with them. They undergo so many pressures within themselves due to hormonal changes that take place in their bodies as they grow. They need help from their parents. 2 Timothy 2:22 *"Flee the evil desires of youth and pursue righteousness, faith, love, and peace, along with those who call on the Lord out of a pure heart."* They do not understand why they have the feelings that they feel. They need the parents to help them go through those changes and how to control themselves. If the parent is ignorant there is no way that he can help the child. Many times, we worsen the situation because of lack of knowledge.

Parents must have time with their children teaching them about life and the ways of God. The biggest problem that we have today is that we have parents who have no knowledge of the ways of God even those who go to church. They do not have active relationships with God. Therefore, there is nothing that they can pass on to their children. Proverbs 22:6 *"Train up a child in the ways he should go; even when he is old he will not depart from it."* Deuteronomy 6:5-9 *"Love the Lord your God with all your heart, with all your soul, and with all your strength. Take to heart these words that I give you today. Repeat them to your children. Talk about them when you are at home or away, when you lie down or get up. Write them down, and tie them around your wrist, and wear them as headbands as a reminder. Write them on the doorframes of your houses and on your gates."* Deuteronomy 4:9-10 *"But watch out! Be careful never to forget what you yourself have seen. Do not let these memories escape from your mind as long as you live! And be sure to pass them on to your children and grandchildren. Never forget the day when you stood before the Lord your God at amount Sinai, where he told me, Summon the people before me, and I will personally instruct them. Then they will learn to fear me as long as they live. And they will teach their children to fear me also."*

If children do not learn to fear God in their lives, then they will not fear any authority in life. Therefore, we have people who have no respect for each other. Husbands and wives cannot respect each other, you go to workplaces, schools, colleges, nations. Chaos is growing every day in the world because people do not have the genuine fear of God in them. The relationship that one has with God teaches him how to be able to deal with other people in a better way. Children need discipline which is a form of teaching. Proverb 23:13-14 *"Do not hesitate to discipline a child. If you spank him, he will not die. Spank him yourself, and you will save his soul from hell."* Proverbs 22:15 *"A child's heart has a tendency to do wrong, but the rod of discipline removes it far away from him."* Proverbs 29:15 *"The rod and rebuke bestow wisdom, but an undisciplined child brings shame to his mother."* Proverbs 29:17 *"Discipline your child, and he will give you rest; he will bring you happiness. A rod is medicine to your child."* There is a difference between spanking a child as a way of teaching him and abusing a child by a rod. Do not abuse a child but he needs a rod to be a better person in life. There is a difference between disciplining a child and fighting with a child. Discipline by the rod should not be done when you are angry it must be administered when you are not angry. You first talk to the child and show him or her why you are giving him a spank. Many parents fight with the child when using the rod, filled with anger. It is not good because you end up hurting the child and you transfer your anger into the child, and this is abuse. We do not spank children every now and then when they have done wrong. Teach them first and if they are repeating the same thing that you have told them not to do then you can spank them so that they may learn. Proverbs 22:15 *"Foolishness is bound in the heart of a child; but the rod of correction shall drive far from him."* If you do not use a rod to drive out foolishness from his heart he will grow into adulthood with that foolishness.

In the world today we have foolish husbands, wives, company directors, foolish presidents of nations, foolish workers, and citizens mostly it is because their parents did not drive out the foolishness that was in them when they were young. They do not want to be corrected because they were never corrected at home. They cannot take a "no" as an answer because no one at home ever stopped them from doing whatever they wanted to do regardless of what harm those things could cause to them. A person who was never given "no" as an answer as a child he or she cannot take it in marriage. Your profession may take you away from your children all the time. Create time with your children so that they may know you and you know them. Many parents are living in the same house with their children, but they do not know each other. As parents, we should be role models to our children but because I do not have time with them, they end up getting some role models from the internet, television because they are always with those people through the media. Our children are getting their values from the internet from people whom they do not know and whom they have never met in person.

Some children have been initiated into witchcraft through the internet some into prostitution the list goes on. Our children can grow up as orphans and yet we are not yet dead. Just giving food and clothing and shelter to our children is not enough, they need us to give them direction in life. If you check today because of the internet, you find that families do not have time for fellowship together. They may all be sitting in the lounge, but each family member is on his own gadget chatting with someone in America, the mother is chatting with some-one in UK the son with someone in Canada, the father with his friend in Kenya the daughter with her friend in Australia. They are all in one room, but they have nothing in common, they are divided, there is no time for each other. Parents are the first teachers of our children, they are exposed to us first before they get into the wider community of the world. As parents, we must set the direction that the lives of our children should take before they are poisoned by what they will meet in the world which is mostly anti-God.

Things that are happening in the world is not just happening, there is the devil directing the events of the world. By separating children from their parents, he knows the effects of it. A child who grows up hurting because he misses his parents is vulnerable to the devil that is the sce-nario that he creates. Children must get their visions of life from their parents; the parents are not available and sometimes they are available, but they have nothing to offer because they are ignorant because their parents gave nothing to them as well. Proverbs 29 :18 *"Where there is no vision, the people perish: but he that keepeth the law, happy is he."* Parents who were raised up by parents who did not know God can only pass nothing to their children except the waywardness of the world.

13

Household chores/Duties

Welcome to house chores, a question which I am asked in men seminars by married couples, they want to know who is responsible for what, division of labor in the home. There is nowhere in the bible where it is written that a woman must wash plates or a man has to do this and that. I might be mistaken if you know where it is written help me with that information. What I Have seen written in the word are the responsibilities of a man and a woman. We shall see some of those responsibilities. I think understanding those responsibilities will help us to answer the question about the house chores or duties. What I have seen is that these house chores work differently in different cultural practices. What I do in my culture is not done in another. Therefore, we do not have one standard across the board. Each group of people or nation or group of people has their own way of doing such things.

We can now get into the responsibilities of a husband or man in a home according to the word of God. He has the same responsibilities as those of God the Father, therefore he shares the same name with him.

1. He is the head of his wife and family. He is the leader of the family. Ephesians 5:23 *"For the husband is the head of the wife, even as Christ is*

the head of the church: and he is the saviour of the body."
2. Provides for the family. Genesis 22:13 -14 *"And Abraham lifted up his eyes, and looked, and behind him a ram caught in a thicket by his horns: and Abraham went and took the ram and offered him up for a burnt offering in the stead of his son. And Abraham called the name of that place **Jehovah- Jireh**; as it is to this day, In the mount of the Lord it shall be seen."*
3. Must love his wife. Ephesians 5:25 *"Husbands love your wives, even as Christ also loved the church, and gave himself for it."*
4. Protects His family. Psalm 91. 2-5 *"I will say of the Lord. He is my refuge and my fortress: my God ; in him will I trust. Surely he shall deliver thee from the snare of the fowler, and from the noisome pestilence. He shall cover thee with his feathers, and under his wings shalt thou trust: his truth shall be thy shield and buckler. Thou shalt not be afraid for the terror by night; nor for the arrow that flieth by day;"*
5. Leads his family in worshipping God – must leave a legacy to his children of worshipping God so that the children can say – the God of our father . Acts 7:31-32 *"When Moses saw it , he wondered at the sight: and as he drew near to behold it , the voice of the Lord came unto him, Saying, I am the God of thy fathers, the God of Abraham, and the God of Isaac, and the God of Jacob. Then moses trembled, and durst not behold."* God knew that Moses knew the God of his fathers he had seen his fathers worshipping him. That is why God gave that reference he knew he would understand.

These are some of the responsibilities that God gave to a man or husband in the family. We go on to see the responsibilities of a woman or wife in the family. When God created Adam there was no woman, a woman came in later, to me, it means all the chores fell under Adam he had to do everything. He lived alone doing everything until God saw that it was not good for this man Adam to live alone. God saw how things were going, things were not good for Adam. God got a plan to make a helper for Adam. Genesis 2:18 *"The Lord God said, It is not good for that man to be alone; I will make for him a helper comparable to him."* Please take note of the word **HELPER,** we shall come back to it after seeing the responsibilities of a woman.

Responsibilities of a woman /wife in the family.

1. She is the helper of her husband, helping him in every area of his life. The husband failed to carry out all the duties that he was supposed to do. Genesis 2:18 *"And the Lord God said, it is not good that the man should be alone; I will make him an helper meet for him."*
2. Submit to her husband. Ephisians 5:22 *"Wives submit yourselves unto your own husbands, as unto the Lord."*
3. To bear children. Genesis 3:16 *"Unto the woman he said, I will greatly multiply thy sorrow and thy conception; in sorrow thou shalt bring forth children; and thy desire shall be t thy husband, and he shall rule over thee."*

The wife or woman completes the husband, without the wife the husband is not complete, he is not able to fulfill the responsibilities that he was given by God. Therefore, according to my observation, all house chores have to be done by the husband with the help of her wife. The wife is the helper of the husband in every sense of the word. Her purpose on earth is to stand with and help her husband in every area of life and in the home. Whether you are going to have a division of labor as to what duties the husband must do or what the wife must do it all boils down to the fact that the wife is a helper to the husband. The husband carries all the responsibilities to run a family. The wife has been given to help the poor husband to carry the heavy burden that is upon him. However, because people do not have a proper understanding of the order of God many families in the world today are being run by women. The order of God has been reversed, women are leading, and men are helpers. Whenever the balance of nature is reversed, we get disastrous consequences. My school of thought says everything in the home including house chores it's the work of a man, but he has been given a helper to help him in dealing with every issue. To me, the two must do everything together. It means they can assign duties to each other according to how they want it to work but there is no law.

14

Marriage and finances

Once you get married, everything about the two of you should become one including your finances. I got the following definition of marriage from a google search, "It is a formal union and legal contract between two individuals that unites their lives legally, economically, and emotionally." What it means is the two individuals become one. Genesis 2:24 *"Therefore shall a man leave his father and mother and shall cleave unto his wife: and they shall be one flesh.* In many marriages, finances are a bone of contention. You cannot have your money together in common if you are not one in spirit, mind, and language. If you do not trust and have confidence in each other this cannot happen. When husband and wife are not working together financially it speaks volumes of bad things that are going on between the two of them. It means the two are living together outwardly but they are not together inwardly. I am not talking about exceptions, but I am talking in general terms get me right.

If the couple do not truly love each other with the love of Christ, they cannot have their finances together. When you are not in one spirit and in mind you cannot be one when it comes to your finances. Husband and wife who are egocentric cannot have their finances in common because the moment they do that they clash because each wants his or her desires to be met. No one between the two is ready to give up his or her desires. Therefore, I said earlier on in this book that we need God in our families. Without God, it is difficult or rather impossible to deal with our egoistic feelings. With all the satanic teachings promoting this ego-centric feeling, that is why husband and wife are just living together as partners, but each person is doing his own things, managing his or her finances with the other one not interfering. If one brings more money in the house, he thinks he has the right to override the other person.

Money is very powerful; it can control your marriage instead of you controlling it. If you check in many circumstances many marital problems, they are caused by a misunderstanding on money issues. I have been a marriage counselor for many years and that is what I have discovered. This is happening in Christian marriages and in non-Christian marriages. On Sunday they come to church, and they seem to be united but when it comes to money each is doing something that does not concern another. Acknowledge that all that you have belong to God .Job 1:21 *"And said, naked came I out of my mother's womb, and naked shall I return: the Lord gave , and the Lord hath taken away; blessed be the name of the Lord."* When you know that all that money you are getting its being given to you by God, then you will not look at who is bringing in more or less . This takes profound knowledge of God not just someone who visits a church building on Sundays but does not have God living in inside of him and guiding him every day. Do not live a competitive kind of life. There is so much competition in the world today, the world has become a race arena. People are always competing, and the acquisition of material things has become the objective of life. Life is becoming unbearable and boring because of this competition. Live according to your means and do not try to live a life that is beyond your financial means. The devil has lied to the world and the world has believed him. He has told people that having a lot of money, cars and good big houses will give us joy and happiness. People cannot be happy now they are waiting to be happy or to enjoy life when they have more money and material things, but this is the lie of the devil. Money and houses are just mere things that do not have life in them. Something that has no life in it cannot give you joy, happiness and peace. Joy and peace are spiritual you do not find them through material means.

Get me right I am not saying you should not have these things as a family, but I am saying do not lose sleep and try to gain money and material things competitively, it will destroy your family. Many couples are spending hours and hours at work trying to make money so much that they are failing to have time to have quality sex. Both are at work many hours, they come home both exhausted, they cannot have sex. This may bring infidelity in the marriage in the long run. When you are buying things, first sit down together and discuss and see what you want to buy. Ask yourselves this question, do we have the money to buy the thing. If you do not have the money start to work to raise that money. It is better to buy what you want cash than to do it on credit. Proverbs 22:7 *"The rich ruleth over the poor, and the borrower is servant to the lender."* Do not put your family in debt. The system of the devil that is operating in this world is to put people in debt because once in debt he can control you. You are a slave as we can read from the above verse. Debt takes away your dignity as a human being. Have you ever been in debt, I have been? I know that feeling that comes upon you when you are meeting with the person to whom you owe some money. You feel very low and useless, you feel as if you are a lesser being. You are living at the mercy of the lender.

Some couples do not sit down and discuss when they want to buy something. One sees something and just buys and the other one is surprised. This is not proper, first discuss. I am not saying do not do some surprises in your family, no. Do not spend so much money on depreciating things. For example, you find someone buying a very expensive car, but he does not have a house. It means that a person's order of priority is not good. A car depreciates but a house is an investment. You cannot live in a car with your family, but you can live in a house. Do not be pushed to buy something because your friends have bought something and yet you do not have the funds to buy. You are different from your friends. Do not live to impress other people, just live your normal life. As a family learns to give to God, support the work of God. Proverbs 10:22 *"The blessing of the Lord maketh rich, and he he addeth no sorrow with it."* Help other people in need, give to the poor. This brings the blessings of God upon your family. This causes you to be financially sound. Sharing your finances with God will cause God to open doors for the financial prosperity of your family. Do not ignore when the poor ask for help. Proverbs 21:13 *"Whoso stoppeth his ears at the cry of the poor, he also shall cry himself, but shall not be heard."* You need your family to be heard when you cry to God.

As a family, we need to make wise investments. Your family needs a home, a house, work towards achieving that. Invest in something that will bring money into the family even in times when you are no longer able to work. Learn to save some money, we do not save because we have a surplus, we save from that which we have. If you wait to save the day you shall have surplus you will discover that that day will never come. We need to be wise the devil has put into the world snares and devices to trap people. He has put worldly ways to acquire wealth. 1 Timothy 6:9-10 *"But they that will be rich fall into temptation and a snare, and into many foolish and hurtful lusts, which drown men in destruction and perdition. For the love of money is the root of all evil: which while some coveted after, they have erred from the faith, and pierced themselves through with many sorrows."* This does not mean that God does not want his children to have wealth, no. We should not get wealth through some worldly ways but through the ways of God.

15

Sex

Proverbs 6: 32-33 *"But whosover committeth adultery with a woman lacketh understandin: he that doeth it destroyeth his own soul' A wound and dishonour shall he get; and his reproach shall not be wiped away."*

1 Corinthians 6:18 "Flee fornication. Every sin that a man doeth is without the body; but he that committeth fornication sinneth against his own body."
Hebrews13: 4 *"Marriage is honourable in all, and the bed undefiled: but whoremongers and adulterous God will judge."*

Sex was ordained by God so that mankind can enjoy and reproduce. God honours sex but it must be done accordingly. It must be enjoyed only by married people within the context of marriage. Having sex with someone who is not your wife or husband brings judgement upon you. The word of God says a man who commits adultery with a woman lacks understanding. He lacks the understanding of what sex is all about and what the word of God says about it. Sex was created by God therefore before doing it you must first get understanding from Him. The person who commits adultery destroys his own soul. Adultery brings wounds on the spirit of the victim. Unfortunately, these wounds are spiritual they cannot be seen by the naked eye. The victim gets dishonour, God dishonours him, and he gets a reproach that cannot be wiped out for the rest of his life. This is what happens to someone who sleeps with a wife or husband who is not his or hers.

Sex is more than two people sleeping with each other. Sex is a spiritual thing although it is a physical act. Every person that you have sex with, you connect with him spiritually. Whether you know it or not this is what happens whether you like it or not. Sex is also called sexual intercourse; the word intercourse describes how the two people intertwine and become one person physically and spiritually. As the two have sex they are sharing what is in them physically and spiritually. 1Corithians 6:16 *"What? Know ye not that he which is joined to an harlot is one body? For two, saith he, shall be one flesh."* Sex is a door for spiritual transference. As the two get connected demons are transferred from one person to another. During sex, the two people share what is in them physically and spiritually. Sex is the most effective weapon that the devil uses to bewitch people. Witches and wizards use sex to destroy and take away people's destinies. Most people you see practising prostitution do not do it just to get money, they do it because some of them are in witchcraft. As they sleep with people, they are bewitching them. Divers kinds of sicknesses, diseases, spells, and curses are transferred through sex and marriages are destroyed through extramarital sex.

I was once a missionary in a certain country and witches came to me pretending to want to worship God, but it was not true they wanted to be closer to me so that they could kill me and my wife. When they came and we preached to them Jesus they ended up giving up witchcraft and coming to the Lord, they told us so many things that they do through sex to bewitch people. The witches testified that when they sleep with men, they collect the sperms of the men that they sleep with and take it into the world of witchcraft, and they use it to bewitch people. They said that sperms were in very high demand in the world of witchcraft. The sperms of the person that is collected that person will either become sick or lose his destiny if a businessman his business starts to go down until he ends up with nothing, if married, will end up divorcing. They said they targeted people with great futures and destroy them by sleeping with them. Many people play with sex and sleep around with everyone, it is because they lack understanding and their eyes have been blinded by demons. They are not aware that when they do so they are selling their lives to the devil.

Sex with your wife or husband is honourable before God. It is a gift from God. Husband and wife must enjoy this gift.1 Corithians 7:3-5 *"Let the husband render unto the wife due benevolence: and likewise also the wife unto the husband. The wife hath not power over her own body, but the husband: and likewise also the husband hath not power of his own body, but the wife. Defraud ye not one the other, except it be with consent for a time, that ye may give yourselves to fasting and prayer; and come together again, that satan tempt you not for your incontinency."*

Learn to satisfy each other sexually. Women take time to be turned on, but men are usually ready all the time. Therefore, it takes some training and learning to understand especially the body of a woman. Even if the husband is taught on what turns on a woman the husband must discover what turns on his own wife. Women are the same but what turns one on does not turn on the other. Learn the anatomy of the sexual organs of a man and that of a woman and how they work. When you understand this, it will help you know what to do during sex which enables both of you to be sexually satisfied. To satisfy a man in bed is not complicated but to satisfy a woman demands stamina, knowledge, and experience. Spend more time on foreplay for a woman to enjoy sex. The sensitive parts that cause a woman to enjoy sex are not inside the vagina, but they are outside. When these sensitive parts are touched and caressed, she enjoys it.

Do some regular exercises, run, do some press-ups etc. You must be physically fit because sex demands some strenuous moments. Exercises help you to be able to endure those strenuous moments. Exercises also help the man not to quickly ejaculate before his wife is ready. If the husband ejaculates before the wife, it lives the wife unsatisfied and it is very painful for her. This is a big problem in many marriages. Eat the right kind of food, especially the husband. If you eat junk food all the time the penis will lose its power during sex. Eat healthy food all the time. If you do not know which food is healthy you can check with people like dieticians, they can help you. You cannot have good sex when your mind is full of stress and problems. If you are living in debt and you have different kinds of pressure between the two of you, you cannot have good sex. Sex is driven from the mind, if your mind is steady and free you can experience good sex. Sex is enjoyed with people who are ready physically and spiritually.

Pray for your sexual life always. Demons can get involved in your sex life and disturb it. Sometimes when demons are involved you find every time you want to go to bed the devils bring up a small thing that causes the two of you not to understand each other and you find you go to bed bored, and you cannot do what you had planned to do. If you see this happening more often you may suspect that demons could be involved. Another thing that can happen is every time you want to go to bed one of you becomes sick or feels very tired. Demons can also cause the penis of the man to lose its power during sex or it fails to erect every time during the time of foreplay. Sometimes demons can just cause the husband and wife to lose interest in each other for no reason. When such things happen, the purpose is to destroy the marriage and many marriages are destroyed that way. When I tell people to pray before having sex some people laugh at me. Demons can disturb and play havoc during the time you should be enjoying one another.

Get help and training on how to have good sex as husband and wife. Sex is fundamental in marriage, depriving each other can only drive your spouse out to have extramarital sex. Some people say they do not enjoy sex, why then did you get married in the first place. Sometimes if you find this happening it could be that you have a spiritual husband or wife. You may have some spiritual forces using you without your knowledge, they can sleep with you during the night and you do not realise it but when you work up you have no desire at all for sex. Sometimes you may have dreams of sleeping with some man or woman and when you wake up you have no desire to have sex with your spouse. If these things are happening often, get the help you need to be delivered from those spiritual forces.

16

Spiritual gift or Godly character?

I have seen this happening especially in Pentecostal circles, when someone is looking for someone to marry, they look for someone who is spiritually gifted for example those gifted in preaching, praise, worshippers, etc. It's good but unfortunately spiritual giftings and godliness and good character are separate things altogether. When someone is operating under the anointing of the Holy Spirit it is not him, but God in action. The person does not live under that anointing all the time. You do not need those gifts in the home, they are needed at church; but at home, you need a god-fearing woman or man of God full of the love of God. We do not benefit much from the spiritual gifts in the home. God-fearing is different from being spiritually gifted. A person can be mightily gifted and yet he or she does not have the fear of God in him.

You need someone with traits in her or his character of servanthood. Servants of the Lord and maidservants of the Lord have the fear of God in their hearts. I am not trying to say all gifted people are not capable of becoming servants of the Lord. To become a servant of the Lord takes hard work to be achieved. It is not something that you just get you must work to have it. Philippians 2:12 *"Wherefore, my beloved, as ye have always obeyed, not as in my presence only, but now much more in my absence, work out your own salvation with fear and trembling."* When we see people ministering in any form in church we admire and think that that is how they live their lives, but it is not always the case. The real person is seen when he is not under the influence of the Holy Spirit. You are not getting married to the Holy Spirit but to a person.

One can be a wonderful singer and preacher but character-wise can be a very big disaster. Christians are divorcing because of this cause when the young man sees a sister sing in church, he thinks there is a sister to marry or it can be vice versa. When they start to live together then that can of worms is opened, everything goes wrong. Having the character of God and singing for God or preaching are two different things. What is needed in the home is a wife and a husband with the character of God. It is not easy to discover the character of a person especially when you are not living with him or her. In most cases, people try to hide who they really are, but there are times when they are not able to do that, for example when you put them under pressure. To know a person, check his or her reaction when they are going through pressure, problems, challenges, and when they are angry, usually they manifest who they really are. When everything is going on well you cannot know a person well. A spiritual gift is something that is given to you by God for the work of God. You get it not because you have a godly character. The moment you receive the Holy Spirit he comes with spiritual gifts. Matthew. 10:8 *"Heal the sick, raise the dead, cleanse those who have leprosy, drive out demons. Freely you have received; freely give."* 1 Cor.12:4 *"Now there are diversities of gifts, but the same spirit."*

You need a wife in your home, not an evangelist or praise and worshipper. Get me right I am not saying these gifts are not good, they are very good for the body of Christ but in the home, they are not of many benefits. In the home, the husband needs a wife with a submissive spirit like that of Christ and a husband who loves like Christ. Marriages are not built on spiritual gifts but on love and submission.

17

Some things that you need to be aware of!!!

A. Parents and siblings Once married there is a great shift that takes place between you, your parents, and siblings. If not understood can bring so many problems and issues in your marriage. Your parents occupied position number one in your life but after marriage, that position is taken over by your spouse, your children are second and your parents occupy position number three. Your brothers and sisters used to be number two they move to number four. Your relatives used to be on number three they go to number five. Your spouse occupies the prime position if this does not happen it may destroy the marriage. Genesis 2:23 -24 *"and Adam said, this is now bone of my bones, and flesh of my flesh: she shall be called woman, because she was taken out of man. Therefore, shall a man leave his father and his mother, and shall cleave unto his wife: and they shall be one flesh."* If you are not aware of this shift and your parents and siblings are also unaware this can destroy the marriage so easily.

B. Bloodline curses There are some bad behaviors and some issues that can follow us into the marriages that our forefathers and our parents were doing. What the forefathers were doing could have been caused by spirits or demons. Then you find you get married and these things start happening to you. Identify those bad things and deal with them for example some have gone through two three four marriages they could not have one marriage, stinginess, lying, gossip, dirtiness, extramarital sex, barrenness, etc. Genesis 25:21 "And Isaac intreated the Lord for his wife, because she was barren, and the Lord was intreated of him, and Rebekah his wife conceived." You may deliver yourself from those things through the word of God and prayer but if you cannot seek help from people who know God and who God uses in the ministry of deliverance before it is too late.

C. Cultural Practices. Many cultural practices bring problems in marriage because marriage must be lived according to the word of God. I have seen people getting married according to their culture, but marriage must be lived according to the word of God not according to some cultural practices. Most of these practices are against the word of God. Any practice which takes away the love of God from the husband to his wife should be abandoned and any practice that takes away submission from the wife to her husband must be abandoned too.

God is the engineer of marriage Learn how God wants it to be lived and how to enjoy it.

D. Lies. You may lie for a while but the day your lies are discovered by your spouse you lose all the integrity and trust that your spouse gave you. You lose value to him or her and it will take a long time to build the trust again. Trust is paramount in marriage; all other things are built on trust. No one wants to be connected to a liar therefore, trust is more valuable than money. John 8:44 "Ye are of your father the devil, and the lusts of your father ye will do. He was a murderer from the beginning, and abode not in the truth, because there is no truth in him. When he speaketh a lie, he speaketh of his own: for he is a liar and the father of it". No one wants to live a lier, therefore train yourself to be honest and trustworthy. This has destroyed so many homes. This is why I said earlier on in this book that Jesus is fundamental in marriage. He delivers the spouses from lying without Jesus even if you try not to cheat or lie you just yourself doing it even though you know the consequences.

E. Human being is Physical, spiritual, intellectual, and emotional. A human being is not as simple as we think or see, man is very complicated. He or she is not the body that we see he or she is more than that. Man is three in one, the spirit, the soul, and the body.1 Thessalonians 5:23 *"And the very God of peace sanctify you wholly, and I pray God your whole spirit and soul and body be preserved blameless unto the coming of our Lord Jesus Christ."* The spirit part is the one that is made in the image and likeness of God. Genesis 1:26 *"And God said, Let us make in our image, after our likeness: and let them have dominion over the fish of the sea, and over the fowl of the air, and over the cattle, and over all the earth, and over every creeping thing that creepeth upon the earth."* It is the part that has the capacity to understand and comprehend spiritual things of the kingdom of God. The soul is the part that deals with the intellect of a man his emotions, feelings reasoning sub-consciousness. The body is the physical frame body that we see with the naked eye. Before he or she gets married he goes through so many things physically, intellectually, emotionally, and spiritually, some of those things are negative. When you are getting married, you are getting married to all those positive and negative things that the person went through. The negative things are the ones that bring problems in marriage.

A person who suffered rejection as a child expects a lot from the spouse. Unfortunately, the other spouse does not know that the person thcy are getting married to suffers from rejection. Sometimes it is both they suffer from rejection as they were growing up. Rejection makes someone to be generally very sensitive, overreacts, is easily hurt, fragile, gets angry easily, misinterpret and distorts the actions of other people. "Of course, emotional pain is only one of the ways rejections impact our well-being. Rejections also damage our mood and our self-esteem, they elicit swells of anger and aggression, and they destabilize our need to "belong". Unfortunately, the greatest damage rejection causes is usually self-inflicted." **https://deas.ted.com.** If then one is married to someone who suffers from rejection you need to know how to handle that person if you do not know it means there are endless problems in that marriage if they don't quickly go for counseling.

A spouse may have an inferiority complex. This can come upon someone as a result of being constantly being bullied or being told always that he or she is not smart, is not intelligent, etc. The person underwent mental and emotional abuse as they were growing up. This condition triggers many other conditions in a person that makes him or her unstable emotionally and psychologically and this will be loaded upon the spouse. The spouse is not aware of all these hidden traits, what he or she can see is the beautiful shape structure of the body. Another may have a superiority complex; this comes because of emotional pain. The person is emotionally hurting and because of that pain, the person acts in ways that hurt others. You are getting into marriage with such a person. These things cannot be seen with a general eye, you need the eye of wisdom which we can only get from a strong relationship with God. These are things that we need to know before we say to someone "Till Death Do Us Part." The majority of us quickly make marriage vows without really knowing what we are doing. People enter the marriage covenant with people whom they know very little about or even nothing at all. They think they know the other person only until they start to live together on a day-to-day basis. The things that people go through as they grow up have very big effects on the relationships that the person has with other people.

One can get into marriage with someone who was in a marriage that failed because the spouse had some extramarital affairs. The trust of that person has been destroyed in the previous marriage therefore when they get into another marriage the person has trust issues and this will strain the current marriage. The spouse is still seeing his previous partner in the new partner. The partner projects what she experienced with the other partner to the current partner. We are getting married to people who are loaded with past hurts, but many times we are not aware of the facts. The spouses are loaded with negative things from their past. They have been made who they are today by those experiences. The problems that the spouses start to experience in the marriage are usually coming from their past, but they are not aware of it. They start to argue on very small matters, and they wonder why the other person is reacting so violently, and they cannot get an answer. What has happened is not the reason of their fight, that small issue only acted as a trigger to the anger that had been bottled up in the other person because of past hurts.

It is impossible to find someone who is perfect who does not have any negative things that they went through in life. All people have gone through some rough times, therefore what we need to do when we are getting someone to marry is to try and understand what the person went through before we met them. This will help you understand how to handle the person. The person might be very nice looking physically but how is he or she spiritually, intellectually, emotionally. A human being is not the body, the body is just a frame the real person lives in inside. Most young people just look at the body and that is it. This is the source of many divorces in the world today. They try to live together but they discover that the person they thought they were marrying is something else they cannot stand it and they quickly get out of it. People are also followed by some spiritual forces which most of the time are not aware of.

Some women have spirits of men upon them. If you get married to such a person there will be fighting always in the home because the spirit that is in the lady does not want to submit to another man. It is the same with men there are some men who have spiritual women in them. The man behaves like a woman, and he cannot live with a wife because the woman in him will be fighting the wife always. This is where the issues of gays and lesbianism emanate from. A man who has a spirit of a woman in him will want to get married to another man, vice versa. The issue of gays and lesbianism is spiritual, those in it do not realize that they have some spirits in them controlling them. They think it is their choice, but it is not, they are driven by the feelings in them that they get from the devil without them knowing. Mostly those spirits got into them when they were young growing up. This is why we need God in our marriages because we are normally loaded with both of us who are getting married with past hurts with things also from our forefathers. We need God to be delivered from those things otherwise after a while we will get divorced

Dr. Francis Madzivadondo is a seasoned Pastor, ordained in 1990 after three years of training in Biblical Studies and Christian Leadership at Africa Multination For Christ College [AMFCC] in Zimbabwe, a bible college for Forward In Faith Ministries International church.

He holds the following qualifications:

-        Diploma in Biblical Studies and Christian Leadership [AMFCC] Zimbabwe Harare.
-        Diploma in Community Services – Australia.
-        Advanced Diploma in Counselling and Psychology – International Careers Institute – Australia.
-        Bachelor's Degree in Christian Education.
-        Master's degree In Christian Education
-        Doctor of Philosophy in Christian Education – New burgh Theological College -USA.

He is an international Gospel conference and television speaker. He has pastored in many places around Zimbabwe for fourteen years before being sent out to foreign nations as a missionary. He has traveled and worked in other nations as a short-term and long-term missionary. He has worked in Mozambique, South Africa, The Democratic Republic of Congo [DRC], South Pacific Islands of Tonga, Australia, Canada, USA, Belize, United Kingdom. Currently, as the book was being written he was working as a missionary in New Zealand as the National Overseer/National Administrator. DDD

He has written two other books.

1. Pulling Down of Strongholds.

2. The Dynamics of the Word of God.

Dr. Francis Madzivadondo is married to Pastor Sandra Madzivadondo and together have five children and five grand children to date.

* 9 7 8 0 6 4 6 8 5 6 6 9 8 *